Th

Library A to Z

Gary Green and Andrew Walsh.

Illustrated by Josh Filhol.

The Library A to Z

Gary Green and Andrew Walsh.

Illustrated by Josh Filhol.

This work is made available by Innovative Libraries under an Attribution 3.0 Unported (http://creativecommons.org/licenses/by/3.0/) creative commons licence.

Paperback ISBN: 978-0-9576652-9-3

Published by Innovative Libraries, 2014.

195 Wakefield Road, Lepton, Huddersfield. HD8 0BL.

andywalsh@innovativelibraries.org.uk

http://innovativelibraries.org.uk/

Durham County Council Libraries, Learning and Culture	
C0 1 72 85377 05	
Askews & Holts	
027	

About the A to Z

The illustrated letters that follow highlight and celebrate the breadth of services, resources and facilities available through libraries. The services, along with the words that have been turned into these illustrated letters, aren't comprehensive, but are just a representative sample based on a crowdsourcing of ideas in Autumn 2013.

The quotations are extracts from the "Users' Stories" section of the Voices for the Library site, where they can be read in full:

www.voicesforthelibrary.org.uk/stories/

The book, along with other Library A to Z materials were funded through a Kickstarter campaign. The materials can be downloaded at:
http://innovativelibraries.org.uk/libraryatoz

For more information about the services libraries provide, how you can help support libraries and who our Kickstarter contributors are, see later in the book. First of all, please enjoy the gorgeous illustrations and the celebration of our wonderful libraries.

Gary & Andrew.

A is for access; advice; answers; archives; art (view public art and sometimes borrow it too!); astronomy (some libraries loan out telescopes for stargazing); audio books; author events.

Those six little bits of cardboard gave me access to all sorts of conversations I just wouldn't have had without them. They led to me studying academic subjects I wouldn't have pursued otherwise (Latin and Classical Civilisation), kept me curious and enthusiastic and taught me that having eclectic tastes does not have to mean bad or trivial. They taught me to take an active role in my own, ongoing, education.

What libraries meant to me when I was eight years old.

B is for baby bounce and rhyme; biographies (learn about others); Blu-rays; board games; book club; books; borrowing; breakout space; breast feeding (space for mothers with babies); business information.

At a time when banks are closing doors to new and small businesses, the library has become a haven of information to help me work around that. My library card is probably as valuable as a credit card. What it gives me in information, I am going to be able to use to target customers effectively and allow my business to grow. By providing this service, libraries contribute directly to positive local economic growth.

Kristin's story.

5

C is for careers; carers services; childminders; choices; classics; coffee (relax with one); collaboration; colouring (fun sessions for children); comics; community; community cohesion; community memory; competitive advantage (for businesses); council information & services (access to); crafts; creation; CVs.

I am a childminder who lives in a very rural area and do not have wide access or can store the variety of books which schools and nurseries do so I use our public library and library bus. The children are always very excited on library day. Visiting the library provides me with books that help me educate the children about our multi-cultural world and different faiths and show them it's all right to be different. I can find books that help the children understand about different feelings and how to express them.

Carlin's story.

CAREERS

D is for dads; dance; databases; democracy; Dewey; digital literacy; discovery; diversity; download (things that the library buys); dry; dvds; Dyslexia / disability support.

Libraries ensure that everyone can gain access to information and thus partake fully in the democratic process. The role of a librarian is, therefore, absolutely crucial in a democracy. Without this access, constituents can become ignorant of the actions of their representatives and are consequently unable to partake in the democratic process. This is particularly a concern for the poorest in society who cannot afford books, let alone internet connections. Whilst the affluent are engaged with the democratic process, the poor are left isolated and disenfranchised.

Libraries the foundation for a democratic society.

9

E is for Ebook readers; ebooks; education; email (access to); employability; enquiry service; entertainment; equality; escape; events; everyone (is welcome); exciting; exhibitions; expression.

A year or two ago I was visiting one of our housebound readers; an 84 year old, she told me how the library service had saved her life. My colleagues in Stirling Council Library Service had given her access to a laptop and taught her to use the internet and email. When her daughter died, she had the means to keep in touch with all her family wherever they lived and that was critical in helping her cope with the loss.

Helping her cope with the loss.

11

F is for Facebook (access to); families; family history; fax services; fiction; films; free (to join and free books); friends; fun; fundraising; future skills (preparing for the future).

Only child in an impoverished home, never enough to eat, no new clothes or holidays. But the library was free!

Anne's story.

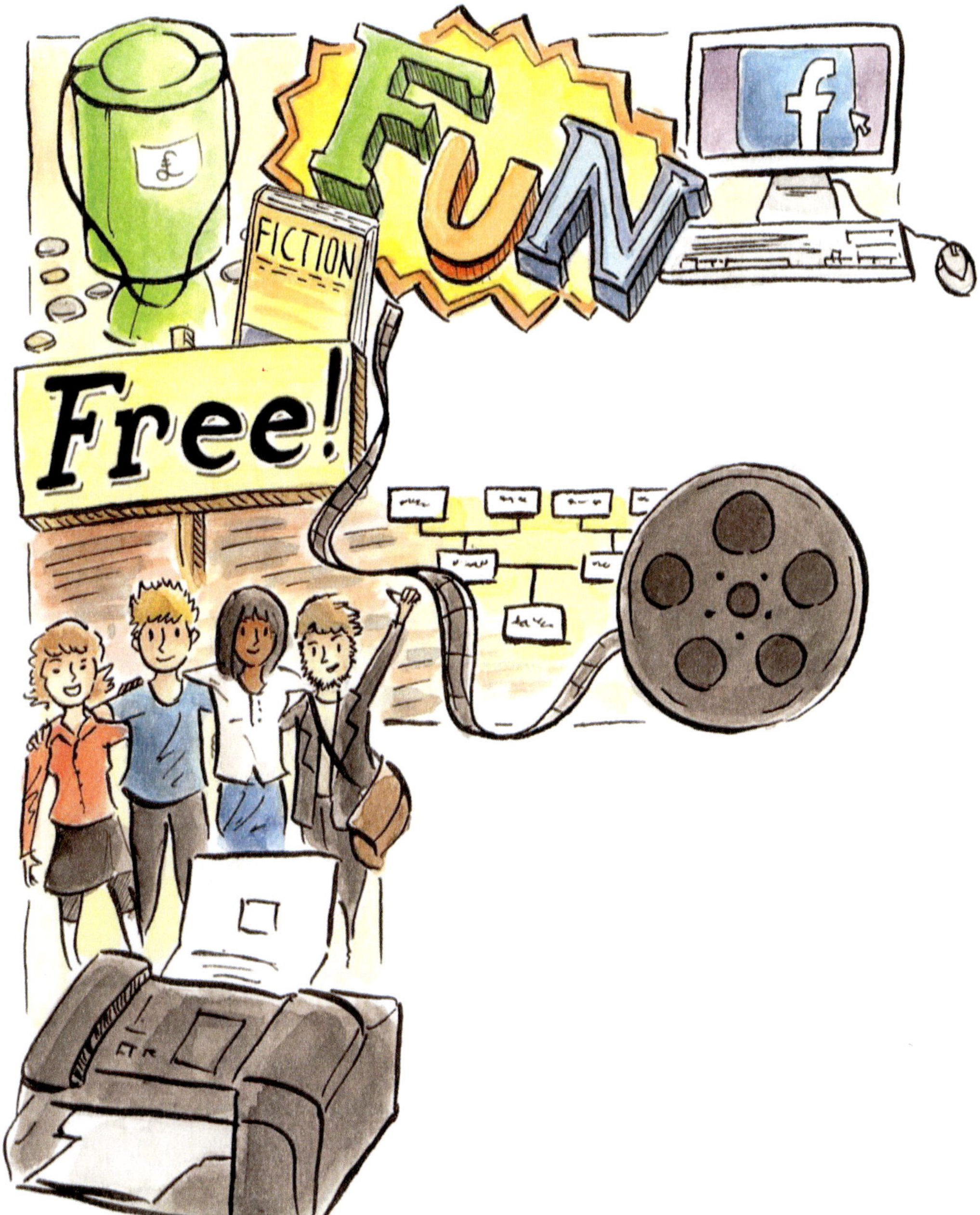
FUN
FICTION
Free!

G is for gallery; games (digital & board games); geographical information; go online; graphic novels; green (eco-friendly book re-use); group work; guidance.

When my husband died my children were 6 and 15. I needed books other than "Badger's parting gift" […] as my husband was in his mid 40s. The children's librarian found about a dozen books for me and for my children at the big book store and they were so very very useful…. meant that the children could read about other children who had lost a parent when they were young. It made a huge difference to us. People think libraries are just about going to borrow books, but there's a great service there.

Irene's story.

15

H is for health; help; heritage; history; holiday reading; home (access library materials from); homework help.

Books on Prescription is a scheme offered by the majority of library authorities, where a doctor or other health practitioner prescribes a book to their patient or service user, usually on a mental health topic. This prescription is then taken to their local library where they can pick up the title, all free of charge.

Read yourself better.

17

I is for images; imagination; inclusion; individual study; information; information commons; information literacy; information services; innovation; inspiration; inter-library loans (borrowing things from other libraries); internet.

When I was poor I always used the internet at the library. It was a lifeline when looking for jobs before having my own computer or the internet at home.

Claire's story.

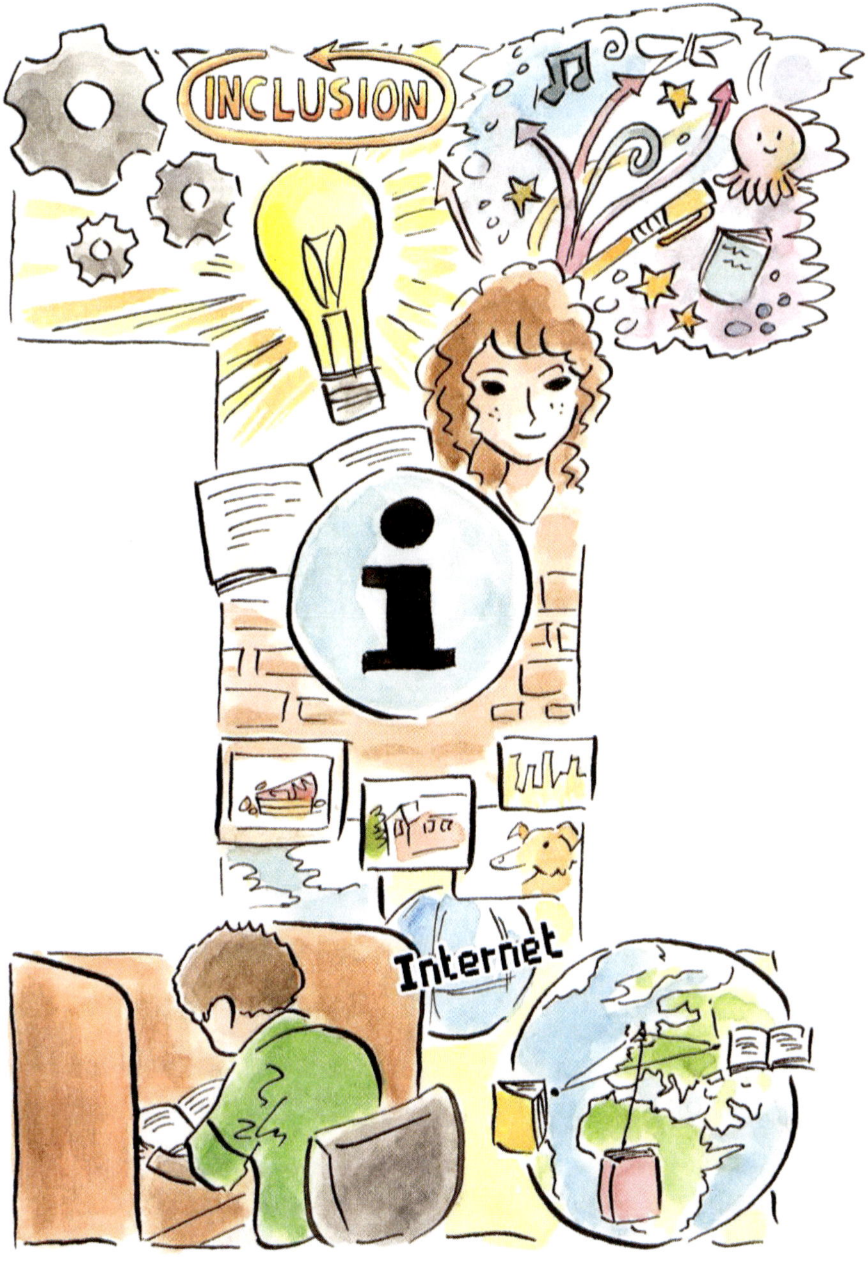
INCLUSION
Internet

J is for job searching; journals; journeys (discover new places with a book); judgement-free.

I was brought up in a 'back-to-back' house with no bathroom and hardly any books. Somewhere around my 8th year I came across this library, a welcoming haven in a large stone-built house. I had never imagined there was so much! The worlds that I found in those books were a revelation; not just the different worlds within the pages, but the fact that those worlds could actually exist at all. Here I found Jules Verne, Homer, Arthur C. Clarke and Jonathan Swift. More important, I found Lilliput, space travel, ancient Troy and submarines…

Universes waiting.

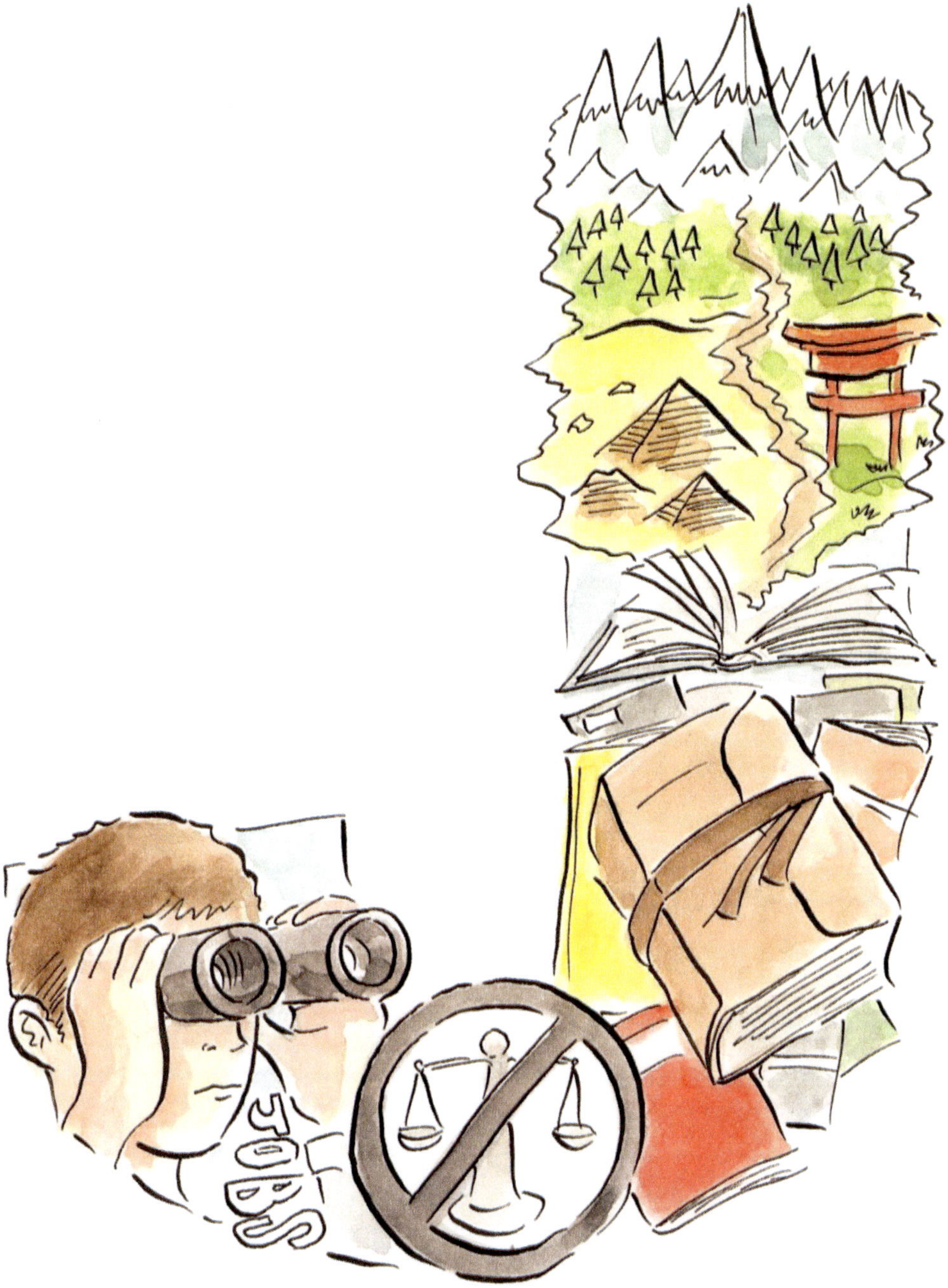
JOBS

K is for key (to success / learning); keyboard (both music & computer); key-stages (support for curriculum work); kids; kindness; kinship; knitting (crafts in the library); knowledge.

The child choosing a book that, for a short time, will belong to him, is learning that knowledge is his, if he wants it. He's learning that it's a right. Libraries set people free.

Libraries set people free.

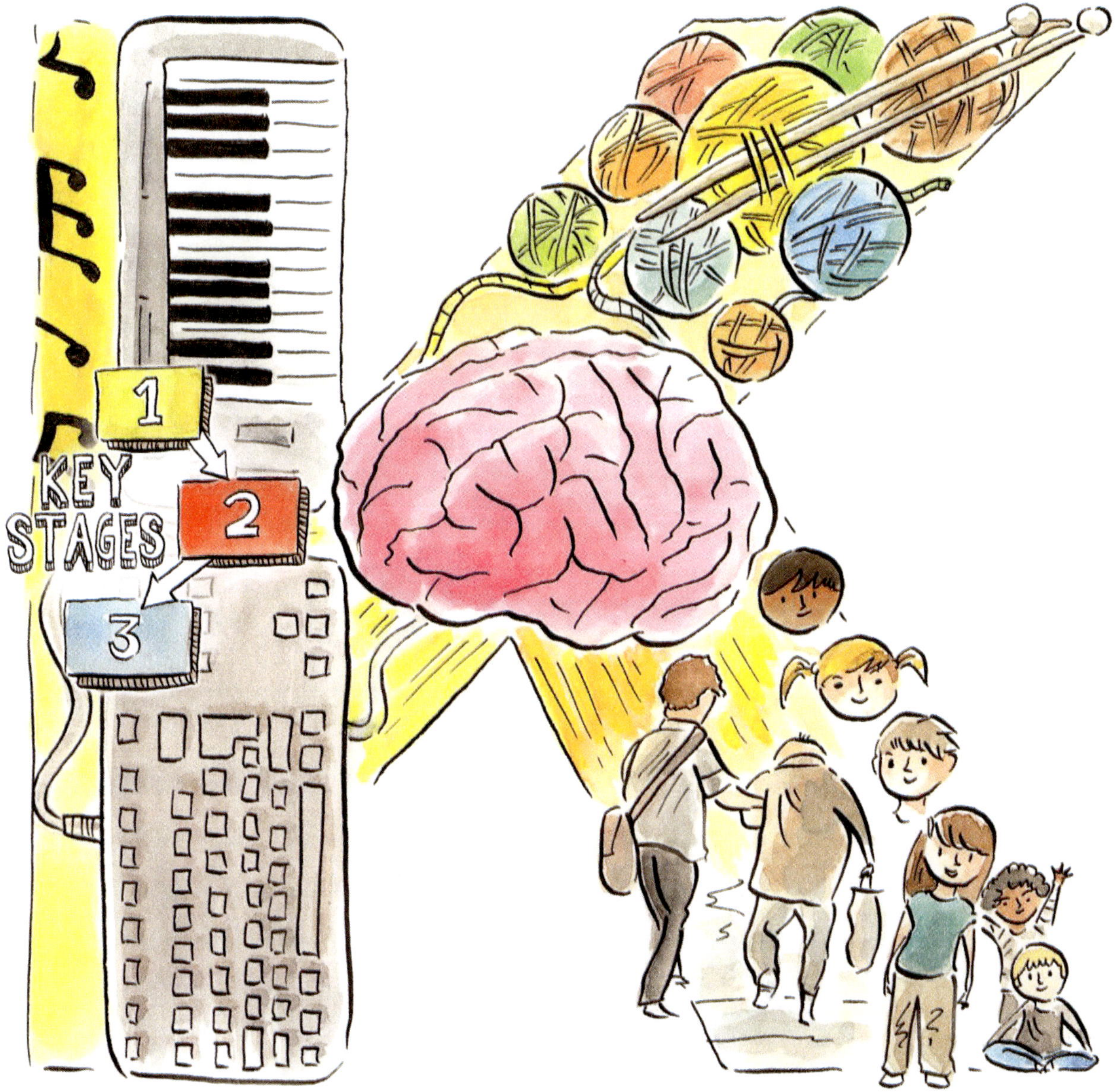
1
KEY STAGES
2
3

L is for languages; learning; leisure; lending / loans; librarians / library staff; literacy; literature; local studies; local to users.

I was desperate to learn French, to be the best in French. So, every day, after school, I went to Doncaster Central Library, took the previous day's copy of Le Monde from its shelf, sat down at a large, rectangular, melamine-topped table and read. On Day One, I understood less than a third of what I read; by the end of the year, I understood most of it (and fell in love into the bargain, with a girl whose name I never found out, who visited the library every day, too). I went on to study German, French and Linguistics at the University of Cambridge

Richard's story.

25

M is for magazines; mailing lists; Make a Noise in Libraries (RNIB libraries campaign); makerspaces; managing directors (building businesses/business support); maps; market research; meeting (business); meeting (community); mental health; minorities welcome; mobile libraries; money saving (free services); mood boosting; mums; music.

Libraries are places where people of all ages, outlooks, backgrounds, incomes, circumstances and opinions meet and mix. By doing this they get to know each other, dispel the demons of difference and realise that, actually, the things we have in common are much stronger than the things that separate us. These are the places where society is built.

Lisa's story.

27

N is for National Libraries Day; networking; new ideas; newspapers; noise (discussion / activity / communication); non-judgemental; not for profit; novels.

Most recently, a reading group... has put me in touch with lively, like-minded folk. Being able to discuss our book choices greatly enriches our reading experiences (whether or not we agree!). The group also provides a much-appreciated social link, which grows more significant for those of us troubled by increasing health problems.

Jan's story.

29

O is for old (and young); online; online resources (databases); open to all; opportunity; outreach.

i am dislexic and have helth problems

i sufer from mentel hellth and haret and allso mobilaty

from the ferst time i came into the libariey about 18 mounths agow

i was hellpt with seting up my computer and given expert hellp to serf the net i was deprived at school wear i never lernt very much

it took me till i was 16 to reed and that isent that good and spelling isent thear ever

this is my dayly activety and socilising wear i can meet frends and have contact with others

i have a son howm is 10 and we go to the libariey to gether on saterday he allso attends school holidays ativatey at the libariety wich he haves so much fun the staff are graiet with the children

Thank you St Budeaux Thomas.

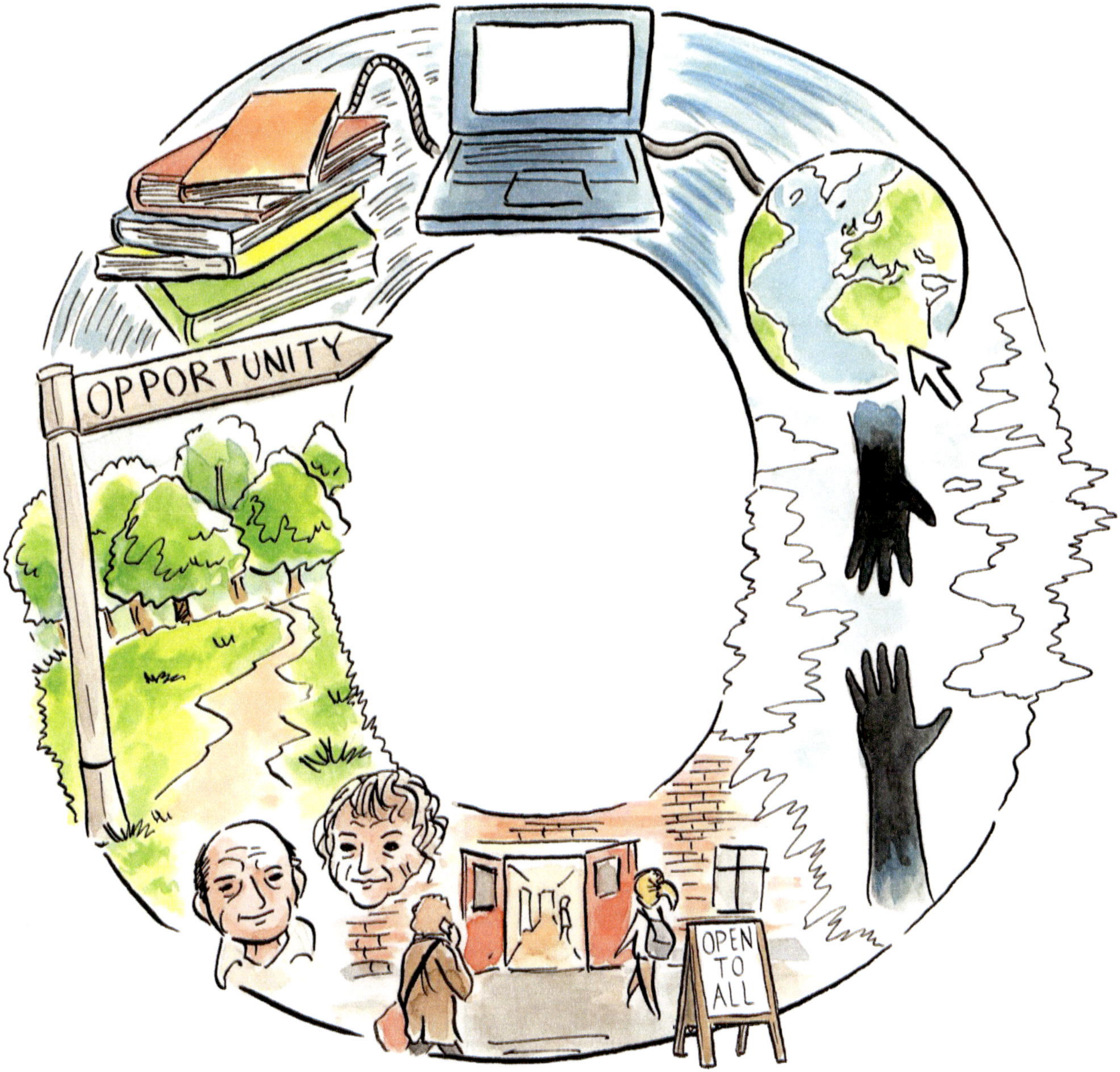
OPPORTUNITY
OPEN TO ALL

P is for paper; partnerships; personal development; photocopying; photographs; pictures (accessing images); political literacy (enabling people to find out about politics in a neutral way); power; printers.

Libraries hold up the lamps by whose light we expand and grow, grant us glimpses into other lives, support our skills and our, understanding, speak across distance and time and race and culture. They hold the keys to civilisation. Let's not let them fail.

Kari's story.

Politics

Q is for questions; quiet.

…public libraries, especially rural ones, are the only way for many people to access knowledge, to access the Internet to inform themselves, to apply for jobs, to be a part of the world outside; the only way for older people to get hold of affordable, large print books, and to continue to be enveloped by human warmth and friendships they may not find at home, and, in turn, to keep their minds and bodies active for longer without having to find refuge in the (also underfunded) NHS. They are prime services of civilisation in an increasingly barbaric age.

Richard's story.

35

R is for reading; recommendations; reference books; references; relaxing; reminiscence; research; resources; retirement; rhyme time.

My five year old daughter has her own library card and gets her own books out. This summer she took part in the Children's Bookcrawl to win a certificate for reading six books and she learned to read using the Oxford Reading Tree books that are kept in the library.

Bryony's story.

Rhyme Time

RESOURCES

REFERENCE

S is for safe (place); scanners; school visits; serendipity; sexual health (information about); sharing; silver surfers; skills; social literacy; social media; spelling; Sshh! (a quiet place to work/study); statistics; stereotype breaking; storytime; students; study; study space (to think and work); summer reading challenge.

What's been most interesting so far are the books that I have found by accident, while looking for something else, that I would have never found in a bookshop or a website. By far the biggest treat has been The Golden Bowl by Henry James, in a beautiful old Bodley Head edition. But there have also been useful books on parenting that I came across while looking in the children's section and fascinating biographies that I found while looking for travel guidebooks. Not to mention the time I arrived with my children to change our books, only to discover a beautiful shadow puppet show was being performed that morning for free.

Polly's story.

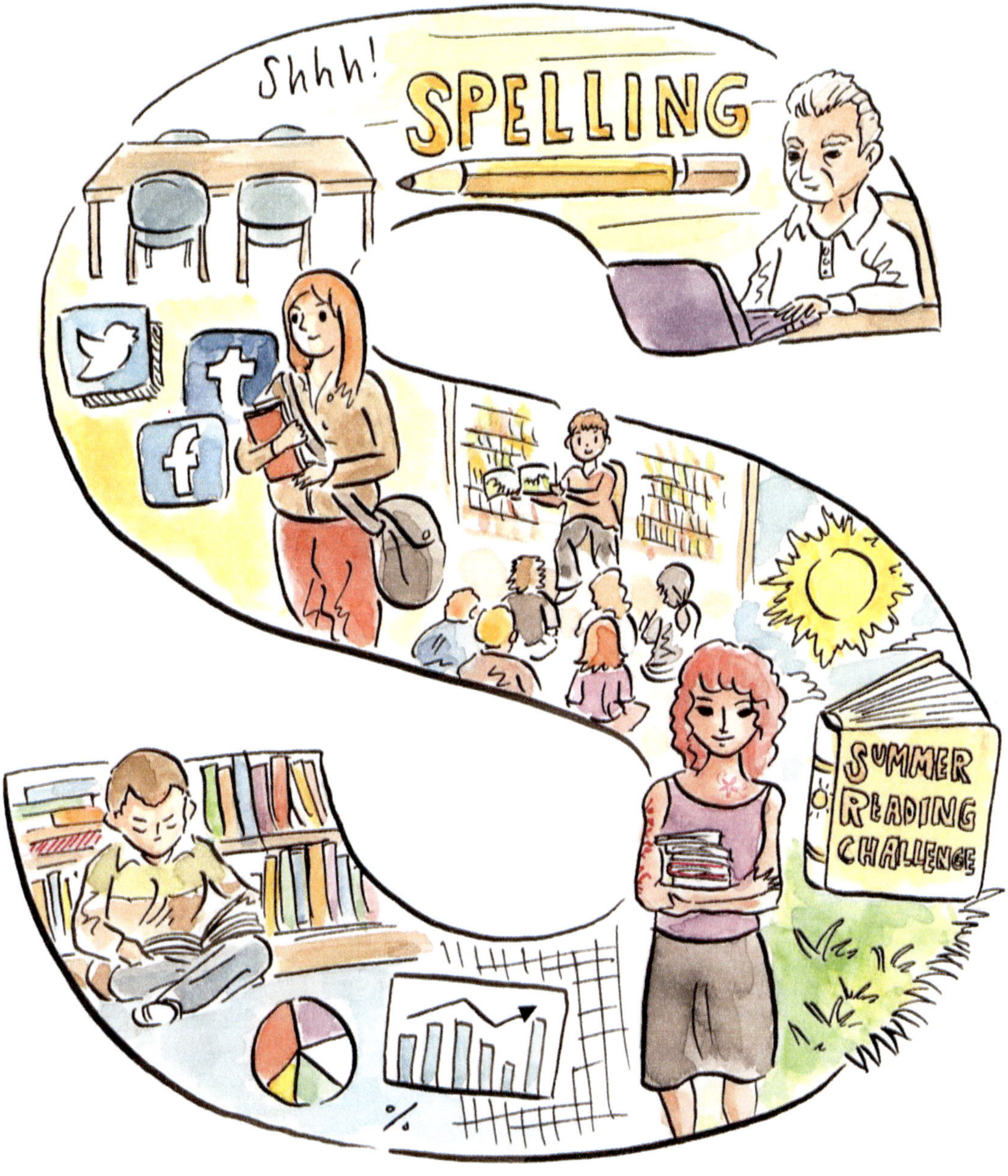
Shhh!
SPELLING
SUMMER READING CHALLENGE
%

T is for tablet computers (e.g. iPads); teachers (supporting schools); teaching / training (librarians teaching); teens; toys; treasure hunts; trusted.

I teach an infant class of mixed ages who always get excited and look forward with great energy to the day that the school library van makes its visit to our tiny village. It is particularly important to our school, and many other small schools, because we do not have a school library.

Daniel's story.

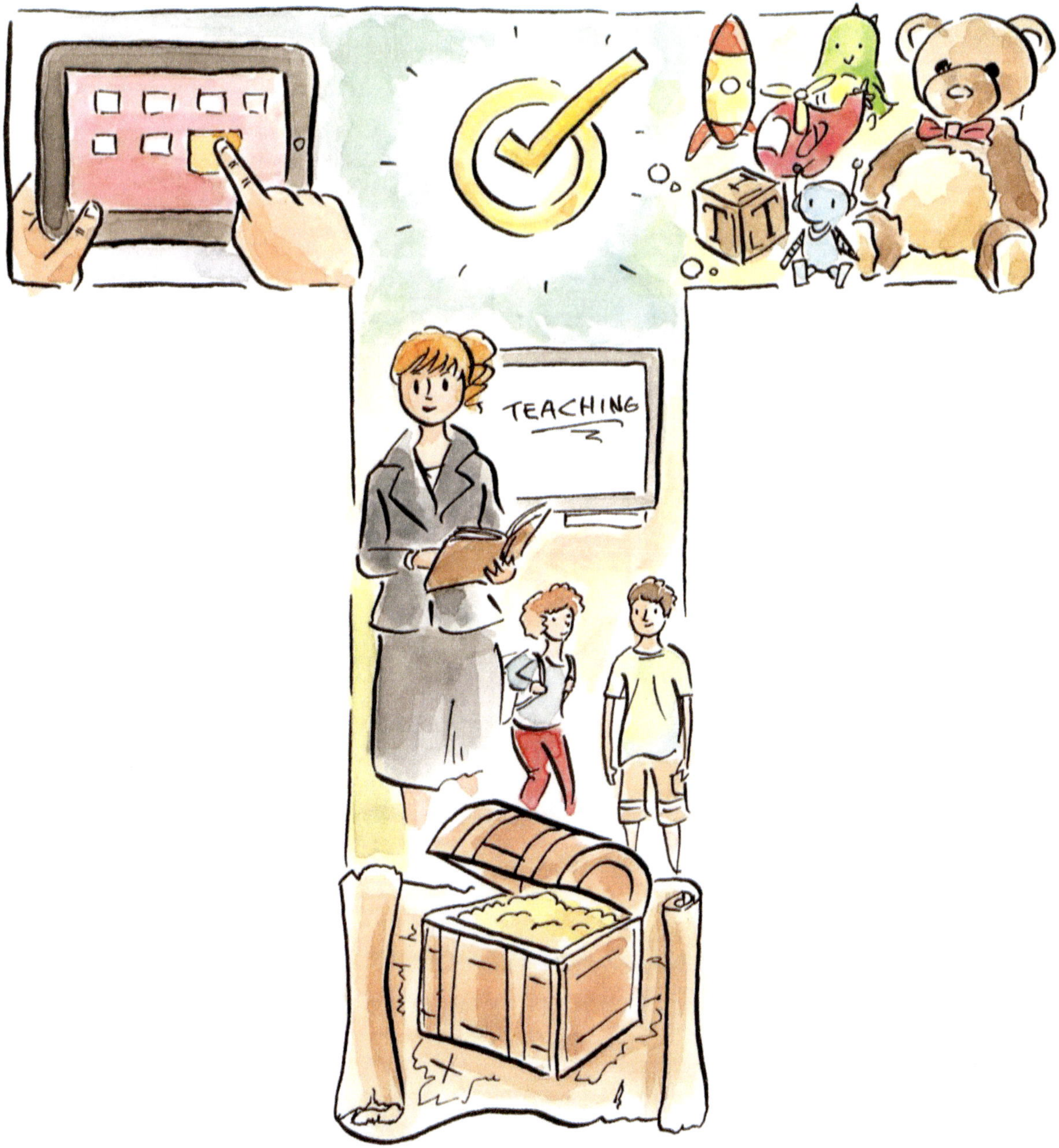
TEACHING

U is for understanding; unemployment (supporting job seekers); unexpected; universal; universal credit (support); unlimited; uplifting.

Job-hunters came in to look at the papers, consult directories, use computers or the photocopier, borrow books and to get a little bit of moral support at a lonely and difficult time.

Lisa's story.

Unexpected

UNEMPLOYMENT

V is for value (money libraries save); values (the things libraries stand for); viewing films & other materials; visually impaired users; voting (finding information on political issues).

Then there's the transcription service, and the team of four women who should be given medals for the work they do for the visually impaired. You name it, they Braille it, then record it as a podcast.

Shush no more.

45

W is for warmth; well-being; wifi (free); wisdom; workshops; World Wide Web.

Our branch provided resources for parents home-schooling their children and for tutors working individually with children identified by the education authority as needing additional support. This is an excellent example of how a public library service has roots in a community and in that community's wellbeing that are much, much deeper than many might initially suppose.

Lisa's story.

47

X is for xml (web of information; organisation of information online), eXciting, eXpression.

A library ticket is more than just an exchange for a book. It's a ticket to adventure, to friendships and stories you will treasure forever and it offers a path into adulthood which will shape your character like nothing else ever could. And every child has a right to that.

Jo's story.

49

Y is for young adult; your library; youth.

The whole experience of a library and actually going into one is something very special in itself. The notion that you can find something that interests you as an individual gives you responsibility and allows you to make your own decisions. This skill is something that is essential to all success – the ability to choose something and follow your own intuition. I still remember, some 20 years ago now, my first school visit to the local library. I loved it, the possibilities and potential to learn about anything. This definitely motivated me to read and want to learn because I was able to read what I wanted. The visit to the library essentially took me away from the regular books within my class and gave me a thirst for reading.

Daniel's story.

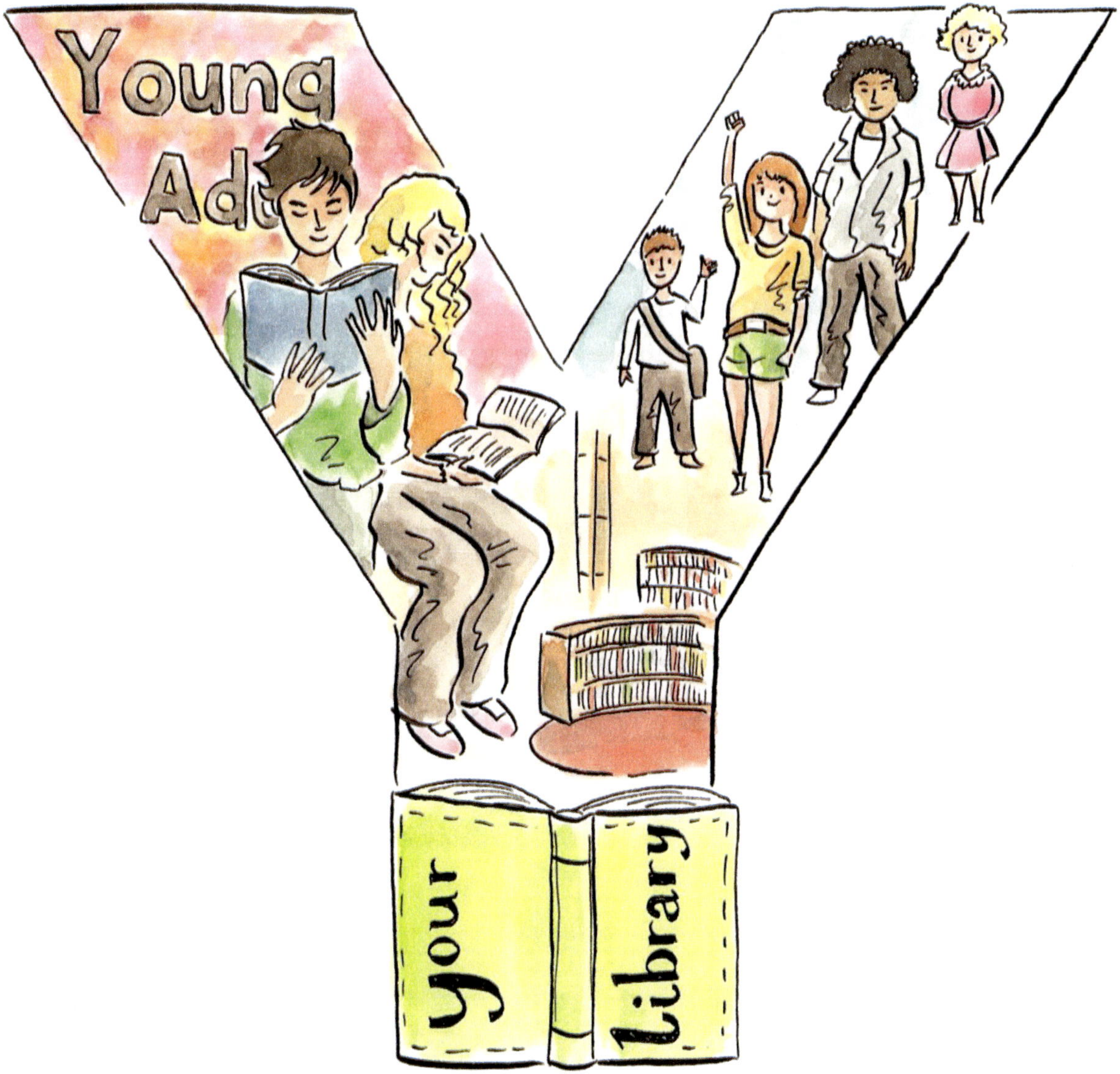
Young
Adu
Your
Library

Z is for 'zines (magazines); zzzzz (child sleeping after being read bedtime story).

Then in came a Dad with two little girls, who were both in their pyjamas. The organiser of our event approached the Dad and offered him the brochure for the photography, the Dad explained he wasn't there for that reason. He proceeded over to the children's section and sat with his two children and read to them what I can only presume to be their usual bedtime story.

Rebecca.

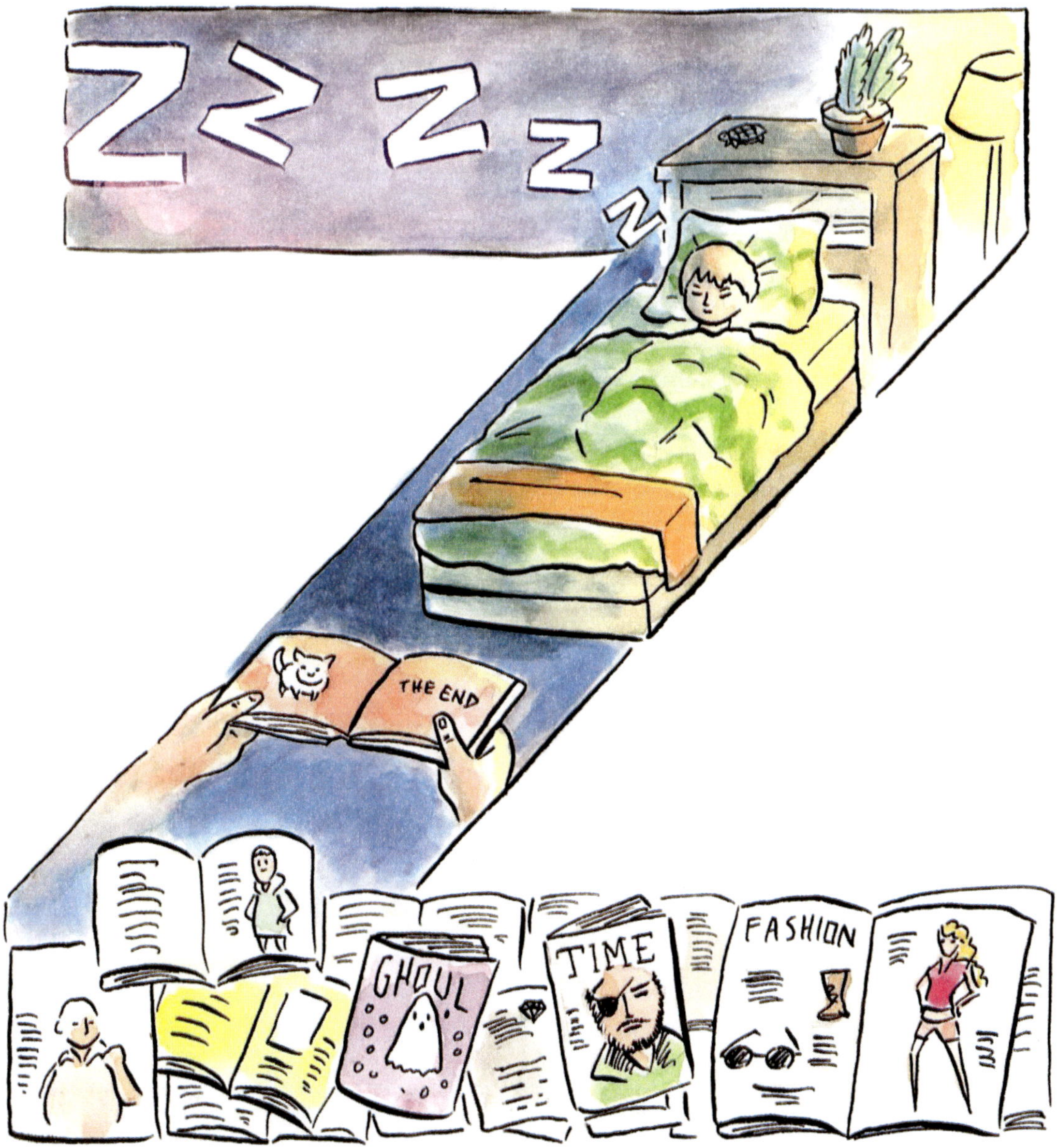
THE END
GHOUL
TIME
FASHION

It's your library – fight for it!

The Library Campaign is proud to be key sponsor of this Library A-Z.

Find out more at www.librarycampaign.com

WHO ARE WE?

We are the ONLY independent national charity that supports library users and user groups.

Our work is carried out by volunteers.

We need your support to do more!

WE KEEP YOU INFORMED

Members receive the ONLY national magazine exclusively about public libraries, three times a year. Check out our back issues on our website.

Our website has daily news updates, advice on running a group/campaigning, useful links and campaign resources, a forum section for your views, and more…

For the very latest news, follow us on Facebook (The Library Campaign) and Twitter (@LibraryCampaign).

WE KEEP THE MEDIA INFORMED

We regularly issue press releases and comments to the national and specialist media.

We are the contact point for local media seeking local library users to interview.

We are the media contact point for comments/interviews on library user issues. Recent appearances include Channel 4 News, ITN Yorkshire, BBC Radio 4, the Bookseller, the Guardian, the Independent, CILIP Update and numerous local radio stations.

WE REPRESENT LIBRARY USERS

We are the ONLY group that sends evidence to government consultations on behalf of library users.

We regularly meet and correspond with the national bodies responsible for libraries, including the Department for Culture, Media & Sport, Unison, CILIP, Arts Council England, the Society of Chief Librarians, MPs and the government.

We have provided core funding to campaigner projects, including judicial reviews of council decisions.

WE LINK YOU UP

Our website has the ONLY national list of library groups, constantly updated as new groups are formed. We can give you advice, and put you in touch with people and groups who can help.

We co-organise the national Speak Up For Libraries conference each autumn.

WE WANT TO DO MORE

We are stretched. We could do more with more members, more money, more time.

Join us!

There has never been more need than there is now!

WE ARE WORTH IT!

Membership fees are kept deliberately low –

£15 for individuals (concessions £10); £20 for groups; £30 trade union branches.

More volunteers are also needed to expand our work. Donations are also welcome.

Our backers!

Many, many thanks to all the Kickstarter backers who made this campaign possible, in addition to The Library Campaign who you can read about on the previous page, the following people backed us financially (and provided us with details for the book):

#uklibchat	@sarahgb	Adele Beeken
Adrienne Rashbrook-Cooper	Alan Fricker	Alan Wylie
Alex Moseley	Alexandra Pooley	Alison Sharman
Mrs Amanda J Ball	Amy Houtenbos	Anabel Marsh
Andrew and Kate Barton	Andrew Strike	Andrew Walsh
Ann Montgomery	Anne Buchanan	Annie Brown
Annie Gleeson	Anon	Dr.Antony Osborne
Anya Dimelow	Arpad Mihaly	Ben Elwell
Bethan Ruddock	Bev Humphrey	Bob Usherwood
Bobbi L. Newman	Brian Rogers	Carlin Anderson
Carol Williams	Chris Barker	Chris Booty
Christina Harbour	Claire Back	Claire Bell
Claire Sewell	Clare Llewellyn West	Cory Doctorow
Damyanti and Owen	Daniel Payne	Dave
David Parkes	Donna Irving	Elisabeth Robinson
Elizabeth Ash	Elizabeth L. Chapman	Elizabeth McDonald
Ellen Forsyth	Ellie Clement	Emily Wheeler
Esther Arens	Fiona Malcolm	Frank Olynyk
Friends of Gloucestershire Libraries	Gaby Koenig	Gary Green & Family
Gwyneth Marshman	Hannah Prince	Helen Blomfield

Helen Murphy	Helen Price Saunders, Cardiff	
Ian Anstice	Ian M Clark	Ingrid Jung
Isobel Blackley	Isobel G. Morris	Jacintha Fid
Jan Holmquist	Jennie Cooke	Jenny Foster
Jenny Meads	Jo Richardson	Jodie Liddell
John Kirriemuir	John McManus	Jon Hardisty
JP Rangaswami	Karen F. Bates	Karly Walters-Smith
Katharine Schopflin	Kathleen O'Neill	Kathryn M Oxborrow
Katie Fraser	Katie Needs	Katrin Roberts
Katy Wrathall	Kirsty Carver	Kirsty Scott (@Kayelle5)
Laura Steel	Laura Woods	Lianne
Linda Moffatt	Lisandro Gaertner	Liz Brewster
Liz Ixer	Lizz Jennings	
Ms Lynne M Coppendale, Proud Librarian		Marie Lancaster
Mark Hughes	Matthew Keable	Megan Dyson
Megan Wiley	Michael Petricone	Mick Fortune
Mobeena Khan	Naomi Nile	Ned Potter
Penelope G Dunn	Pete Smith	Phil Bradley
Phil Segall	Rachel Guilbert	Rachel Spacey
Rebecca Phillips	Richard Huffine	Romany Manuell
Sally Hitchman	Sam Burgess, NHS Librarian	
Sarah Davies	Saskia Hagemann	Shay Moradi (Librarygame)
Steve Thomas	Svend Andersen	Terry Day
The Thomas family	Theresa Morley	Tom Kistell
YiWen Hon		

The importance of libraries

Over the past few years we have witnessed severe cuts in library service budgets resulting in the reduction of services, most notably by closures, shorter opening hours, staff cuts and the replacement of library staff with typically unsustainable and fragmented volunteer-run services. Cuts are often made in the name of austerity measures, yet in austere times libraries are of particular importance to the disadvantaged in our communities.

For many people the word "library" conjures up images of books and not much more. Although books remain a core feature and are beneficial in many more ways than commonly understood, libraries have a much wider and more significant reach than books alone.

With this in mind, in Autumn 2013 we crowd-sourced an A to Z list focusing on the positive impact of libraries [1]. The intention was to use it to highlight the breadth of services available, and celebrate the importance, value and relevance of well-funded and professionally-run public libraries. It is this A to Z that has turned into the illustrated book you are now reading, as well as the related promotional and advocacy material that is freely available for use at http://innovativelibraries.org.uk/libraryatoz . The funding for this book and additional material was raised through a crowd-funding campaign on Kickstarter.com, suggested and organised by Andrew Walsh. All of the generous backers of the campaign are listed in this book.

Through the Library A to Z we illustrate how well-funded and professionally-run library services can help people transform their lives by providing:

- Free borrowing of book stock covering an extensive range of subjects, genres and experiences
- Free access to reference resources, including online subscription services
- The resources to help people educate themselves
- IT classes for people who, for example, don't know how to use a computer, email, or word-processing software, or want to find out about using the internet safely and securely
- Free access to computers and the internet for everyone, including 17% of the British population who don't have access at home
- Support for research using online resources as well as print resources that are not available

- on the internet
- The opportunity to participate in book groups as a leisure activity, or an activity to support mental health and wellbeing, or rehabilitation
- Support for reminiscence therapy for people with dementia
- Further resources to promote well-being, including bibliotherapy
- Spaces for community activities and development
- Homework classes for children who need extra support outside school hours and study spaces for children who don't have a home environment they can work in
- Children's reading challenges and events, which encourage children to continue to read and develop their literacy skills
- Support for job seekers via free access to the internet to search for and respond to job applications, and by helping them to improve their employability skills
- Support to the disadvantaged
- Support for adult literacy initiatives
- Support for community involvement through the provision of information about the local area
- Information for small and new businesses, including research and free access to high cost business information databases
- Information and support to engage with local and national democratic processes, including helping people understand how government works, and providing people with the facts they need to make informed choices about the decisions they are increasingly asked to make about the running of their public services
- A gateway to access further local council services in the library or online, including directing people to further council information

UNESCO emphasises the importance of many of these activities by stating in its Public Library Manifesto:

> "Freedom, Prosperity and the Development of society and individuals are fundamental human values. They will only be attained through the ability of well-informed citizens to exercise their democratic rights and to play an active role in society. Constructive participation and the development of democracy depend on

satisfactory education as well as on free and unlimited access to knowledge, thought, culture and information.

The public library, the local gateway to knowledge, provides a basic condition for lifelong learning, independent decision-making and cultural development of the individual and social groups." [2]

UNESCO also highlights the value of the librarian's role:

"The librarian is an active intermediary between users and resources. Professional and continuing education of the librarian is indispensable to ensure adequate services." [2]

The following facts, figures and quotes from policymaker reports evidence the continued relevance and increasing need for professionally-run well-funded library services in the UK.

Library use

The following statistics indicate the continued significant use of library services in the UK. The DCMS Taking Part survey (2013/2014 Quarter 1) published in September 2013 [3] reported that in England, in the 12 months prior to the survey:

- 36% of adults had used a library
- 16% of adults had visited a library website

CIPFA 2012-2013 statistics published in December 2013 [4] show the continued high-levels of use of UK public library services:

- 288 million visits to libraries
- 42,914 computer terminals in libraries
- 262.7 million book issues
- 21.9 million audio-visual material issues

Literacy and reading

The National Literacy Trust highlighted in their research that 1 in 6 people struggle with literacy; more specifically that their literacy is below the level expected of an 11 year old. [5]

In lower income homes, 14% of children rarely or never read for pleasure. "Just over a quarter of 35,000 children from 188 schools told the National Literacy Trust that they read outside of school." [6]

The Reading Agency emphasises that literacy has a significant relationship to people's life chances.

> "A person with poor literacy is more likely to live in a non-working household, live in overcrowded housing and is less likely to vote. Literacy skills and a love of reading can break this vicious cycle of deprivation and disadvantage." [7]

Libraries are well-positioned to play an important role in improving these figures, through the promotion of literacy and positive reading experiences in local communities, and society as a whole. For babies, children and young people there are baby-bounce, class visits, storytelling sessions, summer reading schemes, and teenage reading groups, including ones specifically focused on Manga and graphic novels, for example. Adults benefit from library groups focused on reading (including specialist groups catering for specific needs), creative writing, self-publishing, as well as reading challenges and author visits, to name just a few of the initiatives. Library staff also visit schools, nurseries, playgroups, prisons and community centres. Outreach is not just crucial in promoting the great work of libraries, and attracting more users, but it can lead to greater community involvement, empowerment and resilience.

Computer and internet use

A common myth that has arisen in recent years is the claim that the internet has made libraries obsolete. However, the multitude of ways in which libraries continue to be used as illustrated in this chapter shows that libraries offer so much more that cannot be provided by a computer with an internet connection. It must also be noted that not every household has internet access.

As previously referred to, The Office for National Statistics reported in 2013 that 4 million households in Great Britain (17%) did not have Internet access. The only way that many people in these situations are able to access the internet for essential services is via free internet access in a public library. [8]

The lack of online access at home also impacts increasingly on children from low income families, who are expected to be able to use the internet for homework purposes. [9]

In the first quarter of 2014 the Office for National Statistics also reported that 6.4 million UK adults (13%) had never used the Internet. [10]

Commenting on the high number of people in the UK without basic computer skills, Martha Lane Fox, the Government's official digital champion, highlighted the key role libraries could undertake to help improve this situation:

> "the government needs to do more: everything matters, from FTSE 100 companies ensuring their workers are skilled to libraries being given the funding to stay open and have computer classes. If we can do this we have a good shot at making a big difference over the next year."[11]

Economic value

With regard to the impact libraries have upon the economy, the June 2014 Arts Council England evidence review [12] commented:

> "…whilst libraries may not 'turn a profit' they provide us with many things that support local economies, from information for businesses, to access to essential text books. Libraries have a local presence and may contribute to a sense of place. Then there are the beneficial effects of services accessed in a library whether that be a social reading club, support to quit smoking, or help looking for jobs online. These are the services that ensure effective and financially efficient public spending and enable us to lead healthy and fulfilling lives."

Further to this the report also comments:

> "…evidence is already sufficient to conclude that public libraries provide positive outcomes for people and communities in many areas – far exceeding the traditional perception of libraries as just places from which to borrow books. What the available evidence shows is that public libraries, first and foremost, contribute to long term processes of human capital formation, the maintenance of mental and physical wellbeing, social inclusivity and the cohesion of communities. This is the

real economic contribution that public libraries make to the UK. The fact that these processes are long term, that the financial benefits arise downstream from libraries' activities, that libraries make only a contribution to what are multi-dimensional, complex processes of human and social development, suggests that attempting to derive a realistic and accurate overall monetary valuation for this is akin to the search for the holy grail. What it does show is that measuring libraries' short term economic impact provides only a very thin, diminished account of their true value."

What the library users say

National library advocacy group, Voices for the Library, evidence the importance of libraries through the stories from library users shared on their site. [13] Users talk about how public libraries serve their communities, promote health, wellbeing and education in general, and more specifically:

- Access to online services
- Addressing the digital divide
- Business support
- Children's services
- Democracy
- Access for disabled users
- Employment
- Equality
- Free services
- Inclusion
- Learning
- Life skills
- Literacy
- Mobile libraries
- Outreach work
- Quality of life
- Reading
- Social cohesion

- Social value

Many of the quotes featured in this book are taken from the stories shared on the Voices for the Library website.

Conclusion

Well-funded and professionally-run library services continue to be important and are of particular relevance in the current socioeconomic climate. However, to ensure that they remain so we ask policymakers, councillors and MPs to take note of this information and act on the manifesto recently produced by the Speak Up For Libraries coalition [14], as follows:

- Acknowledge that libraries provide crucial services, particularly to individuals and communities experiencing hardship
- Give a commitment to engage with communities to design services that meet their needs and aspirations
- Ensure library services are properly resourced and staffed
- A commitment to a service that is publicly funded, managed and run by paid professional staff
- Recognise that properly funded library services contribute to the health and well-being of communities and complement (but should not replace) the work of other public services

And lobby the Government to:

- Give libraries a long-term future, with a vision for their future development and clear standards of service
- Enforce the commitment in law to provide a "comprehensive and efficient" library service. This commitment should also include digital, ICT and e-book services

Gary Green (on behalf of Voices for the Library)

References

[1] Voices for the Library: Get involved in the Library A to Z
http://www.voicesforthelibrary.org.uk/2013/12/a-library-a-to-z/

[2] UNESCO Public Library Manifesto
http://www.unesco.org/webworld/libraries/manifestos/libraman.html

[3] DCMS Taking Part survey (2013/2014 Quarter 1)
https://www.gov.uk/government/uploads/system/uploads/attachment_data/file/244895/Taking_Part_2013_14_Quarter_1_Report.doc.pdf

[4] CIPFA 2012-2013 Public Library statistics
http://www.cipfastats.net/leisure/publiclibrary/default.asp?view=commentary&year=2013&content_ref=17071

[5] National Literacy Trust: Literacy - State of the Nation Research Report (2012)
http://www.literacytrust.org.uk/research/nlt_research/2364_literacy_state_of_the_nation

[6] BBC News: Literacy - Fewer children reading in spare time, research suggests (2013)

http://www.bbc.co.uk/news/education-24387523

[7] The Reading Agency: Reading facts (2013) http://readingagency.org.uk/news/reading-facts003/

[8] Statistical bulletin: Internet Access - Households and Individuals (2013)

http://www.ons.gov.uk/ons/rel/rdit2/internet-access---households-and-individuals/2013/stb-ia-2013.html

[9] BBC: Internet gap hits poorer children, campaigners claim (2014)
http://www.bbc.co.uk/news/education-25729973

[10] Statistical Bulletin: Internet Access Quarterly Update Q1 (2014)
http://www.ons.gov.uk/ons/rel/rdit2/internet-access-quarterly-update/q1-2014/stb-ia-q1-2014.html

[11] Girl Guide: Martha Lane Fox sets out her vision for the future of the digital economy (2013)
http://www.thedrum.com/news/2013/08/30/girl-guide-martha-lane-fox-sets-out-her-vision-future-digital-economy

[12] Arts Council England: Evidence review of the economic value of libraries (2014) http://www.artscouncil.org.uk/news/arts-council-news/now-published-evidence-review-economic-contributio/

[13] Voices for the Library www.voicesforthelibrary.org.uk

[14] Speak Up For Libraries www.speakupforlibraries.org

Further resources

Public Libraries News www.publiclibrariesnews.com

The Guardian: World Book Day – libraries are a lifeline for literacy and social mobility (2014) http://www.theguardian.com/local-government-network/2014/mar/06/world-book-day-libraries-lifeline-literacy-love-books

The Huddersfield Daily Examiner: Lepton Academic Andrew Walsh hopes illustrated A to Z will put libraries on politicians' agendas http://www.examiner.co.uk/news/west-yorkshire-news/lepton-academic-andrew-walsh-hopes-7175587

About the creators:

Gary Green

Gary is a public librarian with a focus on online services and supporting physical library services with technology.

He is also a founder member of Voices for the Library, a national advocacy campaign dedicated to highlighting the value of UK public libraries and the staff who work in them.

Andrew Walsh

Andrew is a researcher and a practitioner, whose work has largely focused on improving the teaching of information skills, especially via the development and introduction of innovative and original means of information literacy instruction. Andrew is particularly interested in information literacy, the use of active learning within library sessions, the application of mobile technologies within the library environment, and game based learning and play in libraries.

Recently, Andrew set up a new publisher for affordable professional development books for LIS students and staff, with the help of a crowdfunding campaign.

Andrew is a University teaching Fellow and a National Teaching Fellow.

Josh Filhol

Josh Filhol is a Freelance Illustrator based in the UK. In his work he uses a variety of techniques such as pen and inks, as well as digital programs. He enjoys drawing in sketchbooks, creating characters, typography and all sorts of ideas. More of his work can be found on his website: www.jfilhol.com